This book belongs to:

And this is what I would look like if I were telling jokes in a hot-dog costume:

How do lions like their
cheeseburgers cooked?
Medium rawr!

**What's the difference
between a fish and a guitar?**
You can't tuna fish.

How do you eat a hot dog when it's cold outside?

You scarf it down.

What did the zero
say to the eight?
Nice belt.

Why didn't the cookie
go to school?
She felt crummy.

**What kind of haircut
do bees get?**
A buzz cut.

What did the volcano say to his mom?

I lava you.

What vegetable should
you avoid on a boat?
Leeks.

What's a snake's
favorite subject?
Hissss-tory.

What did the big flower say to the small flower?
What's up, bud?

What do you call a head
with no body and no nose?
Nobody knows.

Why was the tomato embarrassed?
Because it saw the salad dressing.

What do ghosts put
on their bagels?
Scream cheese.

What did the crocodile
say to the fly?
Stop bugging me.

What kind of shorts
do clouds wear?
Thunder-wear.

Why was the
ice cream lonely?
Because the banana split.

What animal won't
share the shrubbery?
A hedgehog.

What do you call a bird in a snowstorm? A brrrrrr-d.

How did the pirate win
his basketball game?
With a hook shot.

What do you call a
female crustacean?
A she-shell.

What did the porcupine
say to the cactus?
Is that you, Mama?

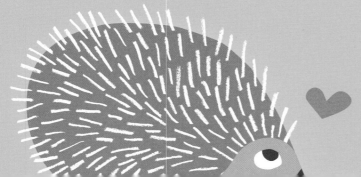

How did the grizzly give directions?

Pad ahead, then bear left.

Where do cows
go for fun?
To the moooo-vies.

**What do you call
a frozen rabbit?**
A hop-sicle.

Why was the
strawberry worried?
Her friend was in a jam.

How did the eagle apologize?
"I'm soar-y."

What do you call
a giant pile of cats?
A meow-ntain.

Why was the broom late for school?

It over-swept.

What did the water
say to the boat?
Nothing, it just waved.

**What kind of tree
fits in your hand?**
A palm tree.

What do you call a bird in a snowstorm? A brrrrr-d.

How did the pirate win
his basketball game?
With a hook shot.

What do you call a
female crustacean?
A she-shell.

What did the porcupine
say to the cactus?
Is that you, Mama?

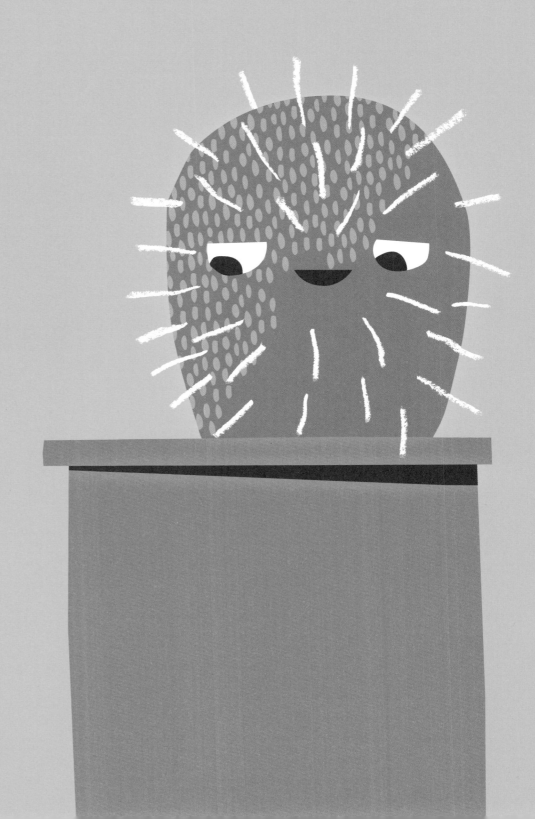

How did the grizzly give directions?

Pad ahead, then bear left.

Where do cows
go for fun?
To the moooo-vies.

**What do you call
a frozen rabbit?**
A hop-sicle.

Why was the
strawberry worried?
Her friend was in a jam.

How did the eagle apologize?
"I'm soar-y."

What do you call
a giant pile of cats?
A meow-ntain.

Why was the broom late for school?

It over-swept.

What did the water
say to the boat?
Nothing, it just waved.

**What kind of tree
fits in your hand?**
A palm tree.

What kind of flower
grows on your face?
Two-lips.

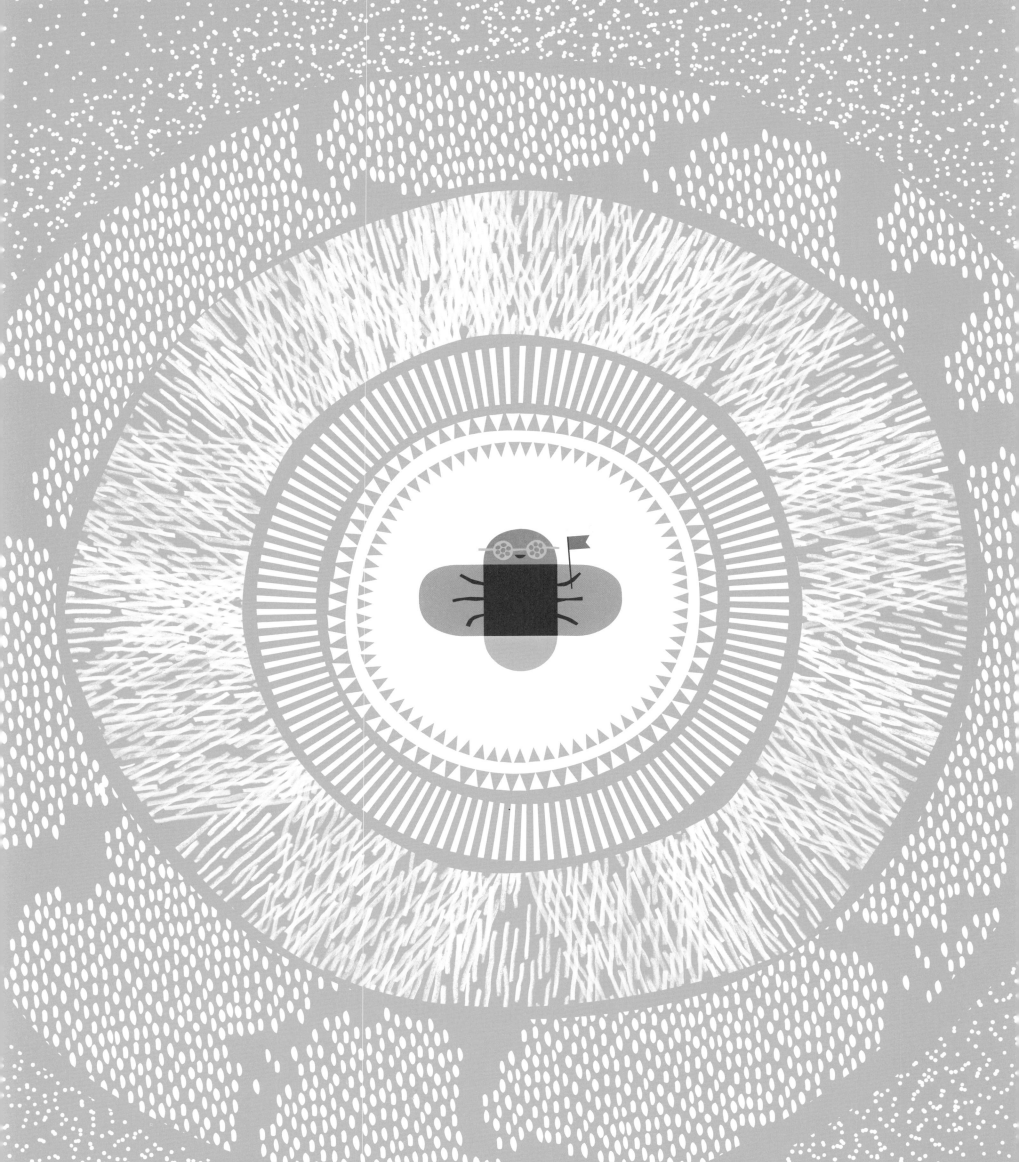

What does a firefly say to start a race?
Ready, set, glow!

What did the mouse
play at recess?
Hide-and-squeak.

Why didn't the skeleton
cross the road?
It didn't have the guts.

Why was six afraid of seven?
Because seven ate nine!

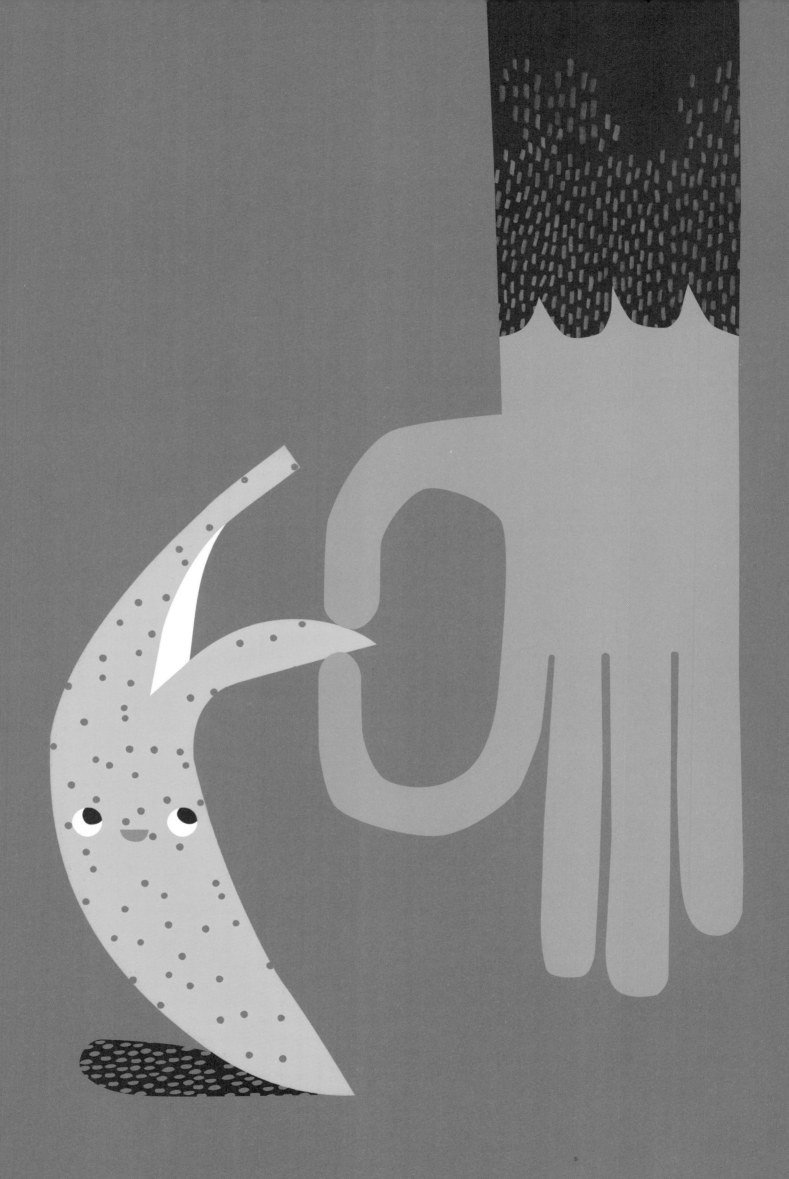

What kind of key
can open a banana?
A monkey.

Where do snowmen
keep their money?
In snowbanks.

Why couldn't the pony sing in the talent show?

She was a little hoarse.

What does a T. rex
do in its sleep?
It dino-snores.

What do you call
a sleeping bull?
A bull dozer.

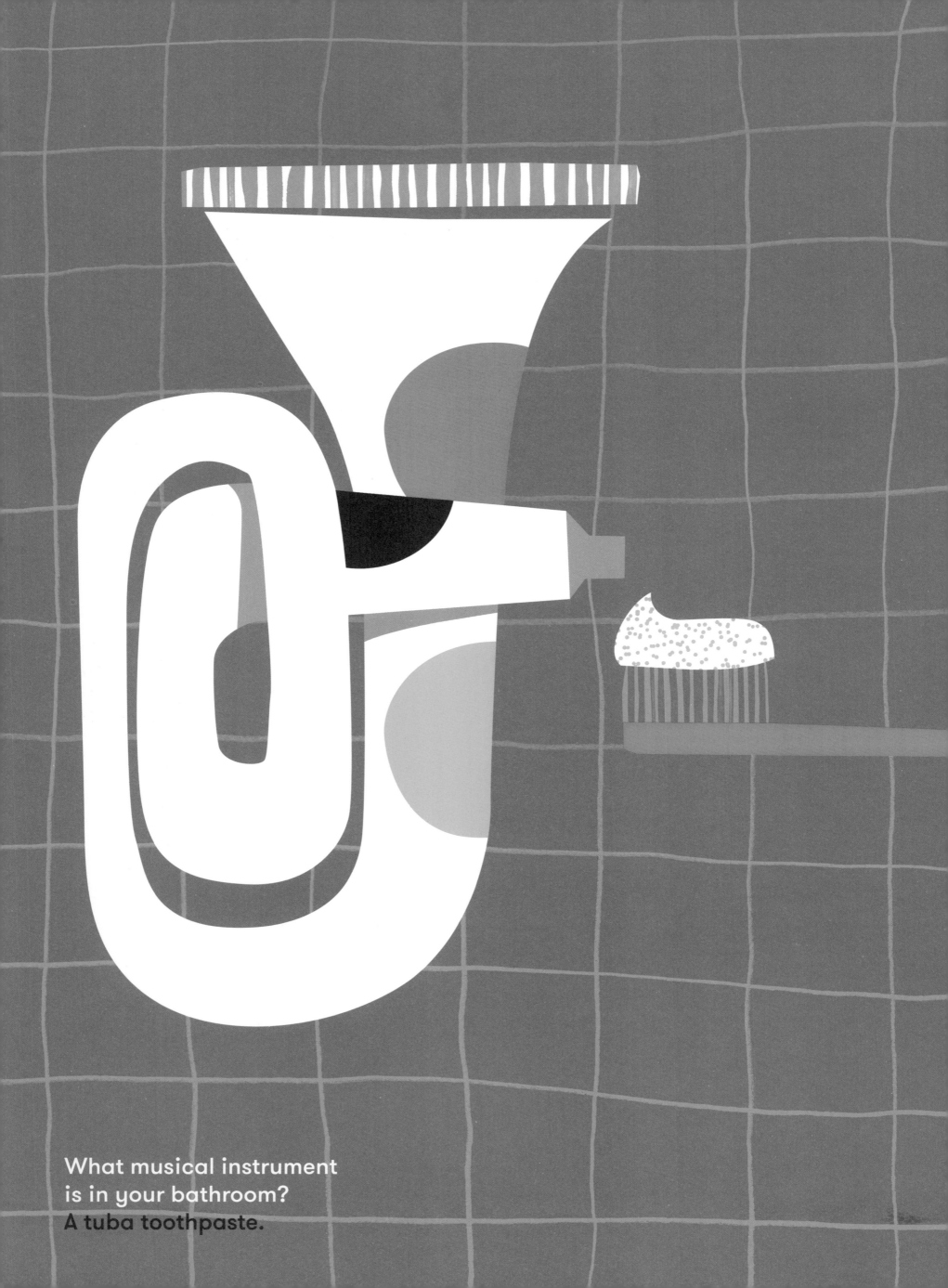

What musical instrument
is in your bathroom?
A tuba toothpaste.

**What do you
give a sick bird?**
Tweet-ment.

How do you organize
a party in space?
You plan-et.

When does an astronaut
get hungry?
At launch time.

What does a coyote
call its vacation?
A howwwwl-iday.

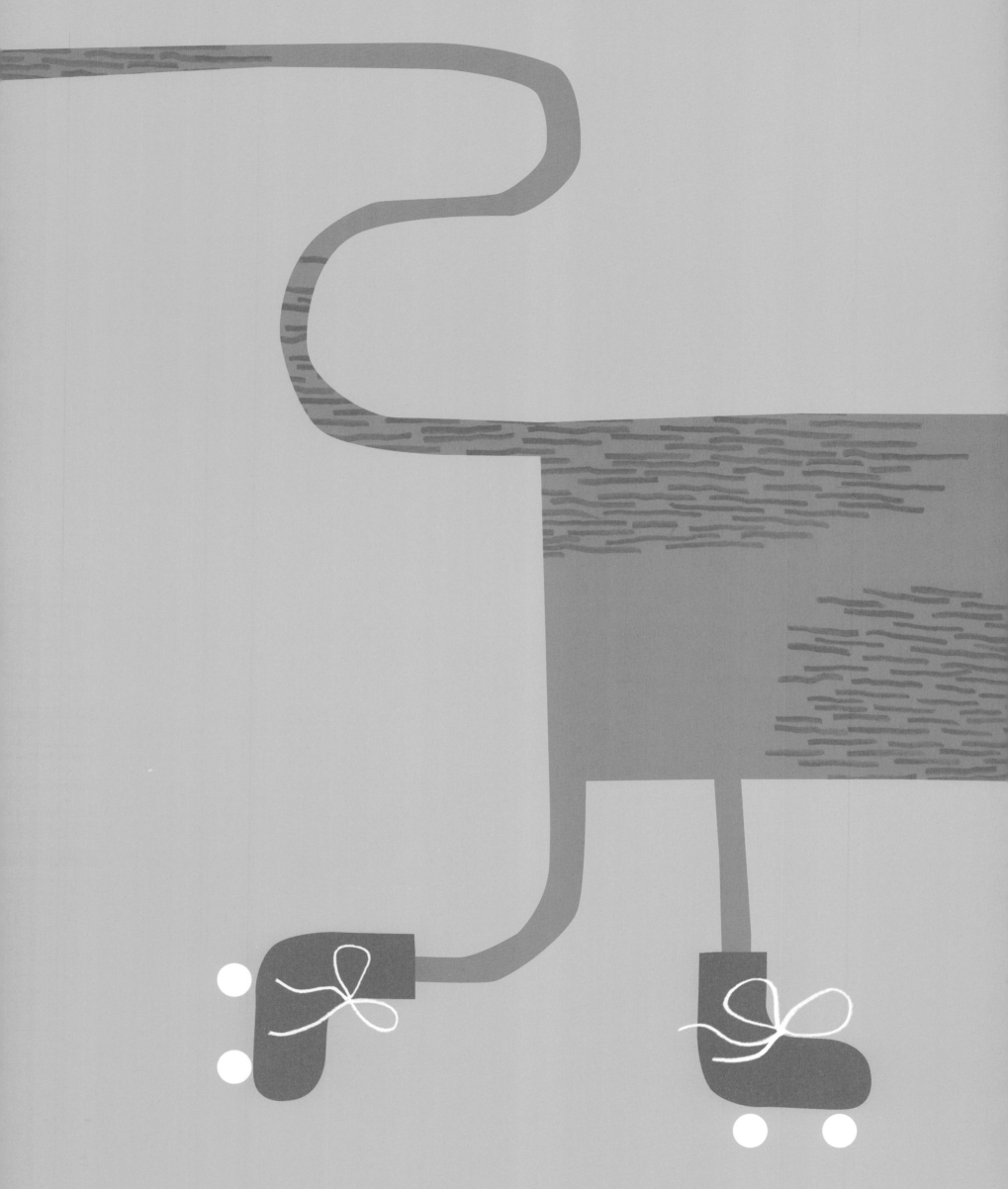

What's a cat's favorite color?
Purrrr-ple.

Why did the house go to the doctor?

It had window panes.

What did the carrot say to
his buddy the mushroom?
You're a fun-guy.

When does it rain money?
When there's change
in the weather.

How did the hamburger
propose to his girlfriend?
With an onion ring!

One more joke . . . This time, create your own illustration.

**Where does a dog ride
a roller coaster?**
At a theme bark.

Illustrated by:

My very favorite joke from this book is:

Reactions I've gotten when I tell this joke:

Name: **Date:**

- ☐ snort-laugh
- ☐ guffaw
- ☐ polite grin
- ☐ delayed chuckle
- ☐ giggles
- ☐ confusion
- ☐ head shake
- ☐ nada

Name: **Date:**

- ☐ snort-laugh
- ☐ guffaw
- ☐ polite grin
- ☐ delayed chuckle
- ☐ giggles
- ☐ confusion
- ☐ head shake
- ☐ nada

Name: **Date:**

- ☐ snort-laugh
- ☐ guffaw
- ☐ polite grin
- ☐ delayed chuckle
- ☐ giggles
- ☐ confusion
- ☐ head shake
- ☐ nada